D1165441

HOFFNUNG'S ACOUSTICS

Hoffnung's

Acoustics

By

Gerard Hoffnung

SOUVENIR PRESS

First published 1959 by Dennis Dobson

This edition first published 1983 by Souvenir Press Ltd, 43 Great Russell Street, London WC1B 3PA

Reprinted November 1983
Reprinted November 1985
Reprinted September 1988

ISBN 0 285 62611 6

My grateful thanks to the following owners of copyright for allowing me to quote, without malice, various musical fragments: Messrs Hinrichsen Edition Ltd (Rustle of Spring, *Peters Edition*), *United Music Publishers Ltd* (Clair de Lune), *Boosey & Hawkes Ltd* (Danse Sacrale *from* Le Sacre du Printemps), *and Alfred A. Kalmus Ltd* (Wozzeck). *G.H.*

For

DR HOWARD FERGUSON

Printed and bound in Great Britain by WBC Ltd, Bristol and Maesteg

The Keyboard

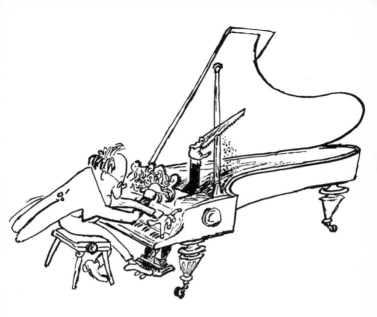

Liszt

Schönberg

A Fugue

de Falla

Boulez

Webern

The Art of Listening

Presto. ($\text{♩} = 132$)

mezza voce

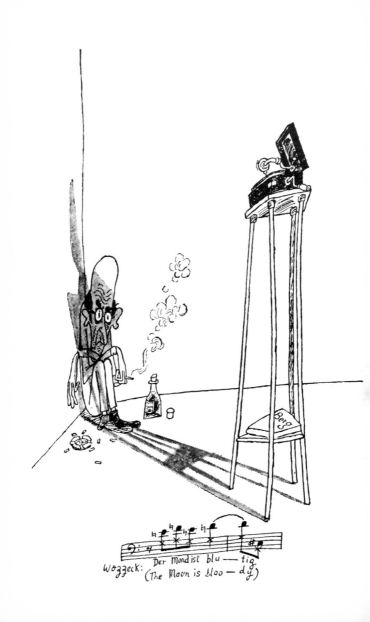

Wozzeck: Der Mond ist blu — tig.
(The Moon is bloo — dy.)

Piano

PP con sordina

Musique Concrète

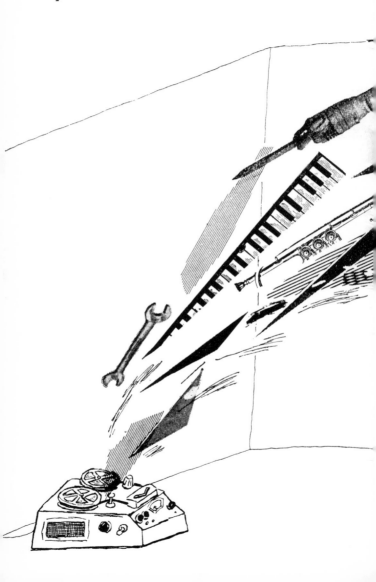

Noises

A Staccato

A Legato

A Crescendo

A Diminuendo

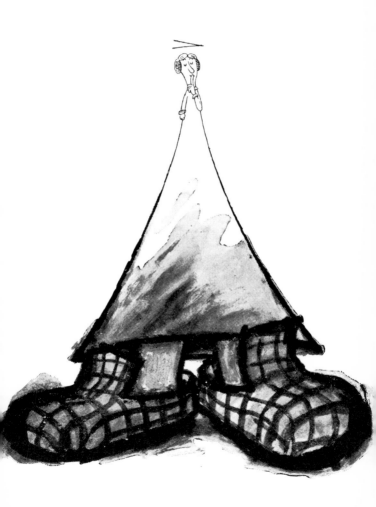

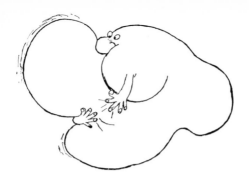

A muted Blow

An Oompah

A Pizzicato

A Rest

A Cadenza

An Arpeggio

A Drum - roll

A Ping

A Thud

A Chord

A Discord

A Hum

A Glissando

A Tutti

Union Members

ƒƒƒ ƒƒƒƒ

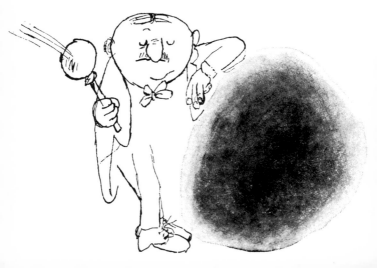

END